Circle of Friendship

By Bob Mumford

LIFECHANGERS ®

P.O. Box 3709 ❖ Cookeville, TN 38502
931.520.3730 ❖ lc@lifechangers.org

The Scripture quotations contained in this book are from:

The New American Standard Bible®, Copyright © 1960, 1962, 1963, 1971, 1972, 1973, 1975, 1977, 1995 by The Lockman Foundation. *The Amplified Bible Old Testament* copyright © 1965, 1987 by The Zondervan Corporation. *The Amplified New Testament* copyright © 1958, 1987 by The Lockman Foundation. Used by permission. *The Holy Bible: New Living Translation*, Wheaton, Ill.: Tyndale House, © 1997. T*he New Testament in the Moffatt Translation* by James Moffatt, Hodder and Stoughton, 1913-1935. *The Message: New Testament With Psalms and Proverbs*, by Eugene H. Peterson, Colorado Springs, Colo.: NavPress, © 1995. *UBS Handbook Series,* United Bible Societies Copyright © 1961-1997. *The Darby Bible,* PC Study Bible formatted electronic database. Copyright © 2003, by Biblesoft, Inc. *The Letters of St. Paul,* the Arthur S. Way translation Copyright © 1953, Chicago: Moody Press. James Strong, *The Exhaustive Concordance of the Bible* (Electronic Ed. Ontario: Woodside Bible Fellowship, 1996).

PLUMBLINE

Published by:

LIFECHANGERS ®
L I B R A R Y S E R I E S ®

P.O. Box 3709 | Cookeville, TN 38502
(800) 521-5676 | www.lifechangers.org

All Rights Reserved
ISBN 978-1-940054-06-3

© 2014 Lifechangers
All Rights Reserved
Printed in the United States of America

Circle of Friendship

Contents

Model of Friendship...5

Slaves or Friends? 8

Friendship: Rare and Valuable 8

Four Ingredients to Friendship......................11

Application of Friendship...............................12

The Nature of Friendship................................15

Barriers to Intimacy...18

Four Basic Needs 20

Self-Protection and Control 22

What Can We Do?..25

The Necessity of Knowing God 28

The Problem with Triumphalism...................29

Becoming a Father-Pleaser 31

Pleased or Not Pleased 34

Love Like That...35

Walking in *Agape* 37

Jesus Pleased the Father..................................39

The Rewards of Waiting on God 43

Not Always Our Timetable.............................44

He Acts as We Wait 46

Waiting Is a Skill..51

Circle of Friendship

by Bob Mumford

This *Plumbline* is about relationships–our friendship with God, with our spouse and children, and with each other. In it we will look at the four ingredients of friendship and the circle of friendship the Trinity enjoys with each Other. The end result is that we are being invited into a relationship that was modeled by the Trinity. This vertical relationship affects every one of our horizontal relationships—our marriage and family, work, and friends.

We will also see that pleasing God is behavioral. God is *Agape*; therefore, His Kingdom is ruled behaviorally by our motivation to learn to love God with all of our heart, soul, mind, and strength.

Model of Friendship

For some years, I have been trying to understand the nature and mystery of the Trinity: God the Father, God the Son, and God the Holy Spirit. The Mystics and the Puritans used to say that God in Himself is a sweet society. They believed that within the Father, the Son, and the Holy Spirit there was a circle of friendship. Many declared that they could tell in their time of worship when they were fellowshipping with the Father, with the Son, or when it was the Holy Spirit. For me this was very fascinating to say the least. My son, Eric, has a very unique insight into the fusion of the Trinity. He recently wrote:

As Individuals, Father, Son, and Spirit are NOT Self-sufficient; Each draws His life and existence and purpose and joy in relation to the other Two and being bound (fused) to the other Two in Agape. The One God, in Tri-unity, is Self-sufficient. However, due to the sacrificial nature of Their shared Love, and the superabundant yield of Their fusion "glory," God needed to demonstrate it and pour it out upon a created "other" – mankind. This is not eros need, but Agape need.

God has chosen to be in covenant (fusion agreement) with mankind in the God-Man Jesus Christ, and have bound Themselves to us "in Him." In the God-Man Nucleus of the Trinity, God and human beings now share one destiny, one fate.

Our minds, spirits, and level of maturity (Greek: *telios*) are not yet developed enough to adequately comprehend this, but we are incrementally growing! Jesus had been walking with the disciples for more than three years, and at the consummation of His time with them He said,

All authority has been given to Me in heaven and on earth. "Go therefore and make disciples of all the nations, baptizing them in the name of the Father and the Son and the Holy Spirit, teaching them to observe all that I commanded you; and lo, I am with you always, even to the end of the age" (Matt. 28:18–20).

I always saw this verse as an *invitation* rather than a commission. We were being invited into a relationship that was modeled by the Trinity. John 15:13-15 says,

Greater love has no one than this, that one lay down his life for his friends. You are My friends, if you do what I command you. No longer do I call you slaves; for the slave does not know what his master is doing; but I have called you friends, for all things that I have heard from My Father I have made known to you.

One way we know that the Lord is allowing us to be His friend is when He reveals His secrets to us. Psalm 25:14 says, "The secret of the Lord is for those who fear Him, and He will make them know His covenant." When Jesus said, "Baptize them in the name of the Father and of the Son and of the Holy Spirit," He was inviting us into a friendship and fellowship with the Trinity.

Slaves or Friends?

God doesn't just give us truth, He models it. The Word became flesh so that we could see it, touch it, and feel it. We know the love of God because it was manifested in human flesh. Jesus said to His disciples, "Have I been so long with you, and yet you have not come to know Me?" (John 14:9). They were exasperated trying to figure out what Jesus meant. But between John 2 and John 15, the disciples were transformed. *Watch the change.* Jesus began by saying that He "was not entrusting Himself to them, for He knew all men" (John 2:23). Then, in John 15:15, Jesus says, "No longer do I call you *slaves* (servants), for the slave does not know what his master is doing: but I have called you *friends*, for all things that I have heard from My Father I have made known to you."

After walking with the Lord for many years I always assumed the highest honor was to be known as the servant of the Lord. But the Lord wants us to be His friend and desires to tell us all of Father's secrets!

Friendship: Rare and Valuable

Most people do not actually have many real friends. When Jesus started His journey with the disciples, one of the goals He had in mind was friendship. He walked with these twelve men and revealed Himself to them. He worked them through a few "relational" problems like calling down fire on their enemies, competing for the best positions, self-confidence, fear of man, and betrayal. When they had learned their lessons, He began to reveal His heart to them, offering them a degree of intimacy that is difficult to grasp. Real friendship involves trust and intimacy, not over-familiarity.

In the Old Testament, there are many Scriptures about friendship with God. Abraham was a friend of God. Scripture also says that about Moses. God did not speak to Moses in parables but face to face as a man speaks with his friends.

When reading the Old Testament early in my walk with the Lord, I wanted to be God's friend like Moses and Abraham were. Little did I realize that God had already opened that invitation to me through Jesus Christ. When I got saved, I found myself "in Christ," as the New Testament calls it, and was welcomed into fellowship with the Trinity. I was welcomed into the sweet society of the Father, Son, and Holy Spirit.

Let's rehearse a little orthodox doctrine. God the Father is not the Son, the Son is not the Holy Spirit and yet they are One. Thus, within the mystery of the nature of the Trinity we have a very beautiful picture of what is called, "the one and the many." This is what is behind Jesus' statement when He says, "If two or three have gathered together in My name, there I am in their midst" (Matt. 18:20). In this Scripture we can see the nature of the Trinity and how they relate to each other. The Son always honored the Father, but Jesus laid His life down for His friends. Jesus says something very sensitive of the Holy Spirit, "When He comes, He won't testify of Himself, He will take the things of Mine and reveal them to you." The Holy Spirit never speaks of His ministry. In fact, we are not even instructed to pray to the Holy Spirit; we should know Them Individually and as One. Technically, we are not instructed to pray to the Son either because it was the Person of the Son Who came to show us how to relate to Father and Spirit and it is represented from His point of view.

I believe that as the Trinity opens up further to us in the future, we will find that inadvertently marginalizing our relationship with any One of the Three is an inadequate understanding of participating in the shared Life of the Three. Father and Son are more familiar to us than the Spirit because their names and identities are anthropomorphic, but this does not make the Person of the Holy Spirit any less God or any less our Friend. In fact, the Person of the Spirit is the One of the Three Who is now with us in this post-ascension/Pentecost age.

The old chorus "Spirit of the living God, fall afresh on me; break me, mold me, fill me use me…" (see also Acts 13:2-4) is still as anointed today as it was when it first came. It is also a form of prayer directed specifically to the Spirit: I believe it is essential for us to pray to "the Helper, the Holy Spirit, whom the Father will send in My name" (John 14:26) and address our "Wonderful Counselor" (Isa. 9:6). The phenomenon of the rare and valuable community and fellowship the Father, Son, and Holy Spirit have is what we are trying to discover and apply.

Four Ingredients to Friendship

All friends are not the same. David and Jonathan were friends. Job had three "friends!" Some "friends" are what I call "God's little helpers." I recently learned something about myself and my own friendships. Everyone thinks that I am a very warm and open person. But I discovered that I have a short wall that people can get over very easily allowing a friendship at that level and making some think they are my close friends. However, just behind that short wall is a very tall one that is almost insurmountable. Europeans are just the opposite. They have a high wall at the outset, and if you can get over that wall, the next one is short. Having realtional walls seems to be common for many people. The reason for the walls is that we have been so injured, messed up, and betrayed that we do not know any other way to safely relate. This results in a surface kind of friendship that yields very little of what we need.

In my reading one time, I came across four ingredients common to friendship:

1. We have to essentially want the same things.

2. We must have freedom of speech and a lack of fear.

3. We must hold each other accountable, if we don't, the friendship will die.

4. We must give and take in mutuality—the reciprocal action of friendship.

If a relationship is always directed *to you* or *from you*, it is not reciprocal. This is true in a marriage relationship as well as church relationships. There are some churches that drain the life right out of you and give nothing back. There are also people who are essentially consumers; they will drain the life out a church and give nothing in return. If you are in a marriage or a relationship that is all one way, find out what is wrong and get it healed.

Application of Friendship

Let me apply these four principles to our relationship with the Lord Jesus. Jesus says, "I hate iniquity and love righteousness" because that is what the Father likes. If we are to essentially want the same things, then we are to hate iniquity and love righteousness.

The second point was freedom of speech and lack of fear. Let me illustrate this between the Father and the Son. Jesus is hanging on the Cross and everyone seems to have forsaken Him. He has freedom and boldness of speech when He says to the Father, "Why have You forsaken Me?" It was not in anger, but He was holding His Father and the Holy Spirit accountable for the appearance of the event.

Have you ever felt there were things you wanted to say to God and never said them? I remember one time the Lord directing me to a hospital to pray for a young basketball player whose jaw was growing faster than his body. Standing in front of the hospital, my prayer was, "Now Lord, I am going into that hospital and I am asking You to do Your part!" It was a man talking to his Friend. I was frustrated because I had been praying for people for so long and they were not getting healed. In obedience, I went into the hospital and prayed for him and God actually healed him. I was thrilled!

The third point was about holding each other accountable or the friendship will die. God has His Ways and Means Committee to hold us accountable for our words and actions. And, He uses all things in our lives to help us mature. If we do not allow God to hold us accountable, we begin to withdraw, cover, and distance ourselves from God and the relationship suffers.

Fourth, we must give and take in mutuality— the reciprocal action of friendship. This is demonstrated in the relationship the Trinity have with One Another. Each gives and receives their very existence to the other Two. The result is fusion

Oneness in the Trinity. When we receive God's *Agape* and then return it to Him in as pure a form as we are capable, we experience reciprocity. And, the more we give, the more we can receive.

John 5:20 says, "For the Father *loves* the Son, and shows Him all things that He Himself is doing." This is the only time in the New Testament that the word "love" is not the word *Agape*. This word "love" in John 5:20 in Greek means *friendship*. The Father is a friend of the Son, the Father likes the Son, and the Father and the Son have a reciprocal relationship. Now the Father says of the Son, because You are My friend I am going to show You all that I am doing. John 17:21–22 says,

> *²¹that they may all be one; even as You, Father, are in Me and I in You, that they also may be in Us, so that the world may believe that You sent Me. ²²"The glory which You have given Me I have given to them, that they may be one, just as We are one.*

This is the evidence that we have been invited into fellowship with the Father, the Son, and the Holy Spirit. John 14:6 says, "I am the way, the truth and the life, no one comes to the Father but by (through) me." This has to do with coming into the Presence of the Father and enjoying a friendship with Him, not going to heaven.

The Nature of Friendship

One of the things that comes with the nature of sin is the desire to *control* things: control my children, control my church, control my company, and control my friends. However, *friendships do not grow with control.* God is calling us into a true friendship with Himself and with men and women in the body of Christ. In the process, the following guidelines may help us to properly relate.

1. *Be totally realistic about people.* There is a deception which says I like them so much that I believe things that are not true. There are helpful people and there are lazy people. If God gives you a friendship with someone, don't try to control it, just be realistic about it. God knew all about you when He called you; there were no surprises. He is totally realistic.

2. *Never lose respect for the person.* No matter what anyone does, always learn to love the *person.* God's friendship is with us irrespective of whether we do something right or wrong. If you have ever done something really stupid, then have grace enough to allow others to make mistakes without losing your respect for them.

3. *Receive each other as in Christ.* When I meet you, I can look for one of two things. I can look for Adam and the old nature, or I can look for Christ and the new nature and find that. Our perspective when we meet someone should be to

look for Jesus in them. See them in Christ and look for the nature of Christ in them—that is in the nature of friendship. See also 2 Cor. 5:16 which says, "Therefore, from now on we recognize no one according to the flesh...if anyone is in Christ he is a new creature [creation]."

4. *Attempt to be there for the person.* Sometimes this may take extra effort. A friend is someone who knows how to *be there.* Please do not quote Bible verses. Remember the freedom to speak and the lack of fear. Each of us needs someone to talk to when we feel like quitting. If someone confides life-threatening fears in you, please remember that the Kingdom is not collapsing. They are probably discouraged and will be all right in the morning.

Judith and I have a couple who are two of our closest friends. They are honest, stable, loving, and confronting. The Lord said to them one day, "Be a friend to Bob and Judith without expecting anything from the relationship." For many years now they have been our friends in the truest sense of the word. There are times when I can bump up against my friend and like a solid rock, he does not move. Everyone needs that kind of a relationship.

5. *Develop the ability to listen.* The awesome power of listening. Have you ever gone to the doctor and before you even have time to explain what was bothering you he says, "OK, take two of these every week and I'll see you next month." The frustrating part is that if he would have just

listened, you would have felt better. You did not need two pills, you first needed someone to understand you!

6. *Recognize and walk within your own limits.* If you are going to be a really good friend, you must recognize when a situation or conversation could endanger your friendship. Sometimes, you have to say that a problematic situation is beyond your realm and should involve other appropriate parties. Recognize your limitations. If it is beyond you, say so, not out of unfaithfulness but in the best interest of your friend.

7. *Pay the price.* Identify with your friends when they are in trouble. We live in a success-oriented society. You don't have any trouble getting friends when you are the cheerleader, have $10 million, or drive a red Jaguar convertible. But when you do something really dumb, they all seem to leave you. Few are the friends who will identify with your failure.

On one occasion, I remember travelling with a fairly sophisticated group of people. Judith and I had two of our children with us and we were in the airport when our son knocked a tall ashtray over. It went, crash! clang! and rolled down the aisle of the airport. He felt all embarrassed. I went over, loved on him, picked up the ashtray and put it all back together because that was my son. His embarrassment was my embarrassment. The temptation could have been to distance myself and say, "Whose kid is that?" About 10 minutes later, his sister was chasing him, he ran into it again and down the hall the ashtray went. He looked at me, and I started to laugh. I thought of myself when I was growing up. I was so clumsy that I could trip over the flowers in the rug!

A friend of mine was sitting with a teenage backslider in a library in Argentina. My friend said to the young man, "I want to be your friend and walk with you." He was a tough kid who had seen all the religious politics and was hardened. The teenager picked a book up from the table and threw it through the plate glass window of the library and said, "Do you still want to be my friend?" The man never batted an eyelid. He said, "Yes, I am your friend, and now you and I are going to begin by cleaning this up and getting this window fixed."

Barriers to Intimacy

Intimacy in a relationship, even in a marriage, is a very scarce commodity and something that we need very badly. What I am about to address is not ordinarily talked about; however, I felt it is a key issue that needs to be addressed in order for us to move on in God.

Intimacy has to do with knowing someone or allowing someone to know you. The word *know* in the Old and New Testament is an intimate word. It is used in "Adam knew his wife" (Gen. 4:1). It speaks of intimacy in a relationship. The Hebrew concept of "missing it" was to be without God or without life! It had a very strong connotation and the meaning of life was not just existence but it had to do with an intimate relationship with or knowing God. There is an increasing hunger in the hearts of God's people to really know Him and to be known.

John 17:3 says, "And this is eternal life, that they may know Thee, the only true God, and Jesus Christ whom Thou hast sent." John 17 is very holy ground—it is the high priestly prayer. John 14, 15, and 16 reveals an intimate time of Jesus with His disciples.

If you are ever feeling disconcerted or feel things aren't going the way you think they should, I recommend that you read these four chapters in one setting. It is especially meaningful if you read them in a different translation than you ordinarily use. Most of us have been taught that eternal life is continuous existence after we get to heaven. But John interprets eternal life as knowing God. He presents knowing God as the goal, not the means to a goal. The journey of knowing God has been a life-long pursuit for me. Almost from the day of my salvation I have had an insatiable hunger to know God. Sometimes I think I really do know Him and other times it feels as if I haven't even begun.

Intimacy is also described in Ephesians 5. Paul is talking about the relationship between husbands and wives and then in verse 32 he says, "This mystery is great; but I am speaking with reference to Christ and the Church." The mystery of the Bride and the Bridegroom is revealed by your relationship with your spouse. I am deeply convinced that many people are spiritually blind because they are relationally blind. 1 Peter 3:7 says, "You husbands…live with your wives in an understanding way, as with someone weaker, since she is a woman; and show her honor as a fellow heir of the grace of life, so that your prayers will not be hindered." This implies that your relationship with your spouse directly effects your relationship with the Lord.

Four Basic Needs

There are four things that represent basic human need. The absence of any one of these will affect us and our approach to life. In explaining them, I want to go from the natural to the spiritual. Understanding intimacy will help us as we seek to follow Jesus. It is very possible to sell everything we have and buy a field in which there is no treasure, so intimacy is a very important part of walking with God.

1. *Passion or intensity.* Every relationship must have passion or life in it. Some people, marriages, and churches are passionless. They are like robots, sterile and perfunctory. There is no passion in the marriage nor in their relationship with God. God

came to us so that we might have life and have it abundantly (see John 10:10).

2. *Security.* We need to feel secure in knowing that God will always be there. Jesus said that He will never leave us or forsake us (see Heb. 13:5). We also need to know that those we are in relationship with will always be there.

3. *Commitment.* It is born in the will. Our culture encourages people to live together without commitment, but people are realizing how fragile a relationship is without it. "Greater love has no one than this, that one lay down his life for his friends" (John 15:13). Jesus laid His life down for us which is evidence of His ultimate commitment to us.

4. *Intimacy.* It is marked by close acquaintance or familiarity of one's innermost or deepest nature. It is a very personal and private relationship as in a close friend. Again, it is about knowing God: "And this is eternal life, that they may know Thee, the only true God, and Jesus Christ whom Thou hast sent" (John 17:3).

Some years ago, I promised Judith that I would not travel or minister for a certain week that we chose together. On Monday, as we sat looking at each other on the couch attempting to "be together" I realized that it's very hard to make intimacy happen! Then Judith said, "You're not really here; only your body is here. You'd rather be out preaching somewhere." Judith is usually quite direct—she hit me right between the eyes, and I was really bent.

I've always taught that truth is negative in its first appearance, and here it was staring me in the face. So I said, "Lord, could You help me? I really want to know how to be intimate." I knew I could not know God unless there was some intimacy with my wife. The Song of Solomon shows us this intimate relationship. Understanding God's mystery of Christ and His Bride parallels the natural to the spiritual.

For most of my Christian life I have put the "knowing" on God saying, "Why don't You let me get to know You?" Suddenly, the Lord turned that around and said to me, "Why don't you let Me get to know you?" Then I had to face the fact that I was afraid of Him. If I opened up to Him, He might make me suffer or send me to India!

When Adam sinned he violated his relationship with God and began to withdraw, cover, and protect himself from God. When God asked him, "Where are you?" He knew where Adam was geographically. God wanted to know where Adam was relationally. He had violated that relationship and the intimacy between them was beginning to die.

Self-Protection and Control

Can you recognize the difference between relief and change? Sometimes all we want is relief.

A man once said to me, "Bob, my wife gave me a hard time the other day, and I was different for 15 minutes." The illustration dramatizes the fact that change is a very difficult thing. The first reason that change is so difficult is because of original sin. A second reason would be learned behavior. It is what we learned on the street in order to survive or what we learned in church in order to be accepted.

External actions are only symptoms of what is going on internally. The world looks at the external, but God looks at our character. Recently the Lord seemed to impress upon me two words, self-protection and control. He was digging around in my basement trying to get at something in my life that hindered our relationship. Both self-protection and control are learned behaviors and barriers to intimacy. Every one of us has developed elaborate escape mechanisms. We know exactly what to do and say when the pressure is on.

How many understand what a childhood vow is? Something happened to you when you were a child and you said, "My mother hurt me, my father hurt me, my uncle hurt me, and no one will ever hurt me again!" Sometimes it happens when you are quite young. Think about a girl who has been sexually abused by her father or brothers. There is more of that happening than anyone can imagine. So she grows up immersed and wrapped in self-protection and control. She makes vows that affect her behavior, preventing intimacy.

Think for a moment about poverty. Some of us were raised in poverty and quietly vowed, "My kids will never suffer for lack of anything!" An interesting thing about being hurt as a child is that we make certain kinds of childhood vows and respond to life in a way that actually violates Christ's command for us to love. If we are going to love, we have to take a risk. The alternative is to become a professional Christian, erect my self-protective barriers and say, "I love you and God loves you." Everyone knows that is a quarter-inch deep! We get so threatened that we try to arrange our life and the people in it so that we don't get hurt anymore. However, most of the time we don't have a choice of the people with which God surrounds us. Following are three ways that we stay self-protected and in control.

Jokes and humor. As soon as we are uncomfortable, we start telling jokes as a protective mechanism. I had a friend who really loved God, but he was personally insecure. Every time we got together he would begin to tell jokes. It was interesting that I could see that in him but not in myself. I was the same way, being the life of the party with a hundred humorous statements. Little do we know that this is a protective device used so that no one can penetrate past our comfort level.

Anger. We control people with our anger or use it as a defensive mechanism when they get too close. We are insecure and afraid that once they get to know the real us, they won't like us or might even reject us. Eventually people start "walking on egg shells" when they are around us.

Religious talk. We are afraid someone is going to get past our comfort level, so we get religious rather than vulnerable. If you ask someone who is religious how they are doing they may say, "Well, praise God! The Lord's good, Jesus is on the throne, and the Holy Spirit is real!" All you asked was how they were doing! The "positive testimony" has almost incapacitated us to communicate as normal human beings. I urge you to be vulnerable, open, and real and get rid of religious cliches.

What Can We Do?

Allow me to give you five lessons, which have been hammered out on the anvil of experience in my own life that have allowed me to experience intimacy.

1. *Repentance of self-protection and control.* You can never know intimacy without deep recognition and repentance of self-protection and control. Like an artichoke, getting free from self-protection may take several layers of repentance because you have to take it off one leaf at a time until you get down to the heart. Ask God to reveal areas of your life that have been wrapped in self-protection and control.

2. *Take the risk.* Growth in intimacy (between husband and wife, friendships, you and God and God and you) involves risk, discomfort, and pain. Self-protection and control are designed to

eliminate the risk. The moment we cease taking a risk, we cease walking in the Kingdom. It is important for you to hear me say that your search for intimacy puts you at risk. It is more than worth it, however, for the alternatives are frightening. By not taking the risk of being intimate and vulnerable with God and others, you actually risk becoming a professional Christian and being alone—all alone!

3. *Relinquish control.* The two major barriers of self-protection and control must be recognized and withdrawn. They are so pervasive and present that intimacy cannot grow without relinquishing our rights to these protective mechanisms. We have to make a choice to relinquish control in four areas.

The first is in the realm of conversation. If you don't control the conversation, they will find out that you only finished sixth grade and then you will be embarrassed. Fast talk is only control. It is possible to win the argument and lose your friend.

The second area is marriage. We must make an actual choice to relinquish control in our marriage. I had a controlling mother, so I was overly concerned that Judith was going to control me. When we are worried about being controlled, we end up controlling others.

The third area is fellowship. When we are spending time together, I choose to relinquish control. One time there were about seven or eight of us in a restaurant and the man who was our host began to order for everyone at the table. He said, "You should have the clams; you should have the flounder…." My choice was to either let him control the whole situation or confront him about it. A few years ago I would have confronted him in a flash right at the table, and then we would really have had some excitement! But it was just a dinner, and God was still God, and things were okay. It didn't take anything away from me to tolerate the situation, and I ate the clams and enjoyed them. My wife said later, "You have really changed!"

The fourth area has to do with allowing God to be God. We must lose our reservations and self-protection towards Him and see Him as an eternal Father. His love in Jesus Christ proves His care. We can stop worrying that He is going to put something on us that would prove too much for us to bear. Perhaps you could say "Father, I want You, I want Your very best, I want to know You." That is a direct route to intimacy.

4. *Self-exposure.* We need to look at conversation, marriage, fellowship, and our relationship with God with self-exposure in mind rather than self-protection and control. For many years, I hid the fact that I didn't finish High School. It really embarrassed me. Since then my efforts to earn my Masters and other degrees have given me a new confidence. When we are in Christ, secure in His love, we can afford to be vulnerable.

5. DEW System: Distant Early Warning System. Ask God for this so that we can be alerted early when we are controlling the conversation or religiously protecting ourselves. The Holy Spirit is faithful, and each of us would be much further along in God if we had obeyed even half of His gentle warnings.

The only way we can experience intimacy is by acceptance. I accept you just like you are; you don't have to do anything. We must choose to surrender self-protection and control. They are the two barriers to intimacy in our relationship to God, in our marriage, as well as in every other relationship. If you have been a strong dominating father or a controlling mother you must choose to surrender and take the risk. We cannot surrender without risk. If you cease taking risk, you cease walking in the Kingdom.

Everyone knows there are many marriages that are hurting—real marriages and good marriages that have commitment without intimacy. There are also many churches without intimacy. If God is going to meet us where we are, we must accept one another in order to remove the barriers to intimacy. The absence of control and the removal of self-protection are the first two steps.

The Necessity of Knowing God

Remember the old TV commercial for Shake 'n Bake? Sometimes I wish getting to know the

Lord was as easy as that commercial made it look. When the Lord reveals Himself to one of His kids, it is actually a lot like shake 'n bake; He shakes everything in your life that is not built on His Kingdom, then bakes you in a refiner's fire until everything that is not of Him floats to the surface so it can be removed (see Heb. 12:26-29).

We can joke about Shake 'n Bake, laugh (sometimes painfully) about being under the dealings of God or having to pass through life's valleys as one of those things you just have to go through. However, to the man or woman who is watching their world come apart or their hopes and dreams go up in smoke the dealings of God are no laughing matter. Most Christians fall apart at the point of God's shake 'n bake, not because they do not love the Lord or do not desire to mature in the Christian walk, but because they *do not understand* what is going on when the shaking and baking begins. We not only *begin* the race, we need to know how to *finish* it. It is an intimate relationship with Father God that keeps us on this journey.

The Problem with Triumphalism

The Church in our century is entering a whole new set of testings and pressures. I remember years ago an astute theologian of a somewhat different persuasion than my own came to a meeting where I was speaking. After the worship service he said to me with genuine concern and understanding, "I believe that Christ is being exalted and that you are sincere." Then he hesitated for a moment and added, "However, I do not believe you see the distinction between Christ's triumph and triumphalism." In the years since his pertinent statement I have had opportunity to do a little research and undergo a few "shake 'n bake" experiences that have brought me to a deeper reality of what he saw in my triumphalism.

Triumphalism is an over confident brand of religious enthusiasm that, disguised as faith and concern for God and His glory, is, in reality, success-oriented and preoccupied with the believer's personal victory. The difference is clearly seen in the Apostle Peter whose apparent concern for Christ's triumph was actually motivated by a fear of what he was about to lose! The Peter of John 21, after his denial and failure, was destined to be triumphant in Christ's triumph because he had been delivered from his own triumphalism. Triumphalism is an assumption of victory based on zeal and personal vision rather than on a biblical calculation of God's ultimate purpose and intention.

The nature of triumphalism can be vividly illustrated by the difference between a 21-year-old Marine second lieutenant fresh out of officer candidate school who has never seen a battle and a 50-year-old master sergeant who is a combat veteran of two wars. Both may be equally assured in their own hearts of ultimate victory in the coming battle, but the attitude with which they approach the battle may be vastly different. The new lieutenant may have thoughts of glory, grandeur, and personal performance in battle. He wants to come out with a promotion and a chest full of medals; the master sergeant knows he will be happy just to come out.

The issue is not uncertainty; it is the reality and nature of the battle in getting the victory. The sergeant knows that ultimate victory will be bought with expense rather than exploits, sacrifice rather than success, grit rather than glory, pain rather than pomp, and, horror rather than heroics. The sergeant knows the triumph will come only when each man is willing to pay the terrible price of victory—"and they did not love their life even when faced with death" (Rev. 12:11).

The young lieutenant may regard the veteran sergeant as "over the hill," overly cautious, or just plain "chicken." The lieutenant's dreams, however, have yet to learn what the sergeant knows about "shake 'n bake."

Becoming a Father-Pleaser

And He who sent Me is with Me; He has not left Me alone, for I always do the things that are pleasing to Him (John 8:29).

And you shall love the Lord your God with all your heart, and with all your soul, and with all your mind, and with all your strength (Mark 12:30).

In the midst of an emotional battle, I locked in on what this meant: The entire Christian life should be and was always intended to be centered in our learning how to be a Father-pleaser. If we set our goal to please the Father, a thousand problems are resolved right off the bat and many of our prayers suddenly seem superfluous. A lot of the bits and pieces with which we struggle both personally and relationally simply disappear because our whole life has now become centered on learning to please the Father. As we study what it means to be a Father-pleaser, keep in mind that when we are pleasing to the Father, we are also rightly related to His other kids.

So, I have been trying to understand, biblicize, and be able to teach how loving God and pleasing Him effects our behavior. If I love God in the manner in which He asked, why would that change my behavior? We all know that behavior is one of the hardest things to change. You can believe all kinds of things, but acting different is a whole new challenge. Biblically, it is the central and intended purpose. This is the meaning and essence of the word Kingdom—we are now responding behaviorally to His governmental purpose!

In Matthew 3:17 Father said, "This is My beloved Son, in whom I am well-pleased." Again in Matthew 12:18 He said, "Behold, My Servant whom I have chosen; My Beloved in whom My soul is well-pleased." It is evident that Father is really pleased with Jesus. Then I linked well-pleasing to another Scripture: 1 Corinthians 10:5, "Nevertheless, with most of them God was not well-pleased." Father was pleased with Jesus but not pleased with Israel, and I saw the Kingdom of God—the terms *Agape* and Kingdom are synonymous. Pleasing God is behavioral. God is *Agape*; therefore, His Kingdom is ruled behaviorally by our motivation to learn to love God with all of our heart, soul, mind, and strength.

When we center our whole being on pleasing the Father, it radically affects our ethical and moral behavior. When the grocery clerk handed me too much change, I said, "Excuse me, you gave me $2 too much." She looked at me like I had come from Mars. I said, "I'm a Father-pleaser, and my Father wouldn't be pleased if I cheated you out of your $2." She was impacted, but I wasn't trying to be spiritual; it was a practical lesson in learning how to please the Father. We are now learning the practical lessons of the fear of God. To be as honest as possible results in experiencing Father's pleasure. He is eager for us to discover this as a Kingdom lifestyle.

Jesus was a Father-pleaser. He did not come to die; He came to do the will of the Father, which included dying. "But the Lord was pleased to crush Him, putting Him to grief" (Isa. 53:10). His death was pleasing to the Father. What pleases or displeases God as a Father is important because it re-establishes a long-neglected truth of biblical purpose in human suffering. When Christ arrived at Gethsemane there was a clash of the will between Father and Son. Three times Jesus asked the same question: Father is there any other way to accomplish this task?

When we ask for anything three times, we have to admit that we are seriously considering the cost that lay before us. After the third time Father said no, Jesus yielded and said, "Not My will but Thine be done." Many of us have walked with the Lord Jesus long enough to know that when the personal cost is evident, yielding is not always easy.

Pleased or Not Pleased

This is My beloved Son in whom I am well-pleased (Matt. 3:17).

After my rather dramatic encounter with the Lord when He stated He wanted my love, I set myself to eagerly learn the skill of being more sensitive to the prompting of the Holy Spirit by asking, "What is it Father?" As an 84-year-old, I am equally eager to declare and impart what I believe to be the Kingdom lessons of pleasing God as a Father for the post-modern youth and new believers who are beginning their own journeys. In trying to learn what is pleasing to God we need to learn to make distinctions. *Agape* is not relative; it is an absolute. We can know when we are pleasing and when we are not, when we are givers or when we are takers. Giving is pleasing, taking is displeasing. It is that uncomplicated and simple. If this idea of pleasing the Father rings your chimes, it will provoke a heart response.

Love Like That

> *Watch what God does, and then you do it, like children who learn proper behavior from their parents. Mostly what God does is love you. Keep company with him and learn a life of love. Observe how Christ loved us. His love was not cautious but extravagant. He didn't love in order to get something from us but to give everything of Himself to us. Love like that (Eph. 5:1-2 MSG).*

Because not many of us are able to love (*Agape*) like that, we need to be born again. Jesus gives us the new birth, which consists of His inseminating the Eternal Seed (1 Pet. 1:23) into us, and we begin to cultivate the *Agape* of God. As we continue to embrace the Kingdom reality of the New Birth, our capacity to be pleasing to Him increases. As we learn to "love like that," we know before the words are out of our mouth that we are injuring someone. Our response to His heart is the cause and motivation for us to begin to change our behavior so that it will please our Father. *Agape* becomes our new standard of behavior (2 Cor. 5:14).

What happens when we don't love like that? Although we are born again believers, there are times when we do not love like that—maybe even a minute ago. When I started to teach and embrace *Agape* as the essence of the Kingdom, I did not want anyone to think that I had it home in my garage. *Agape* has become the most confrontational concept in the entire Bible. In Ephesians 3:17 Paul said that, "Christ will live in you as you open the door and invite him in. And I ask him that with both feet planted firmly on love" (MSG). When we are not pleasing to our Father, we can let Christ be His pleasure. Christ did it all: "If you keep my commands, you'll remain intimately at home in my love. That's what I've done—kept my Father's commands and made myself at home in his love" (John 15:10 MSG). Christ kept all of Father's commandments so He could give them to us. We don't have to worry about all of the commandments because He kept them for us. We now only have one command: *Agape*. (See this stated clearly in John 13:34-35). He gave us Christ to make up for all the crazies so that He could love us and we could love Him. Christ perfectly loves the Father for us.

The Lord's Supper is one of the tools God uses to help us "love like that"—to love God and love others as He loved them. The bread is His body given to us for the unqualified purpose of imparting to us His love; we need it to become Father-pleasers. The cup of wine is His blood given to us for the remission and forgiveness for the multiplied times that we failed to love as He loves. His forgiveness comes without rebuke or condemnation. Seen in this light, the Eucharist takes on family and fatherly overtones that make us want to mature in His love with deep gratitude for His provision.

Walking in *Agape*

Walking in *Agape* requires sensitivity. I saw a refrigerator magnet that said, "Wine is evidence that God loves us and wants us to be happy." Father is pleased when I drink the first glass of wine. He may be pleased when I drink the second one. By the third one He might say, that's not for you. We really can learn that degree of sensitivity so that we are alerted the moment we cross the line. For some, this needed sensitivity might be in the area of going to the movies or eating out or shopping. It could be in many other areas such as finances.

Walking in *Agape* is that uncomplicated; it is a Dad speaking to His kids, "trust Me, son, I want you to know My love for you, My intent toward you. Your brother may not be all that easy to love, but 'build yourself up in the faith and keep yourself in the exact center of My love'" (Jude 21). In the next verse it says, "Go easy on those who hesitate in the faith. Go after those who take the wrong way. Be tender with sinners, but not soft on sin. The sin itself stinks to high heaven" (Jude 22-23). Sometimes it is difficult to be tender with sinners; it is easier to write them off if they don't follow our rules. But that is not the heart of a Father-pleaser.

Becoming a Father-pleaser is best discovered in the biblical idea of abiding. "But you, dear friends, carefully build yourselves up in this most holy faith by praying in the Holy Spirit, staying right at the center of God's love, keeping your arms open and outstretched, ready for the mercy of our Master, Jesus Christ. This is the unending life, the real life!" (Jude 20-21). Jesus taught us what pleases the Father:

If you abide in Me, and My words abide in you, ask whatever you wish, and it will be done for you. My Father is glorified by this, that you bear much fruit, and so prove to be My disciples. Just as the Father has loved Me, I have also loved you; abide in My love (John 15:7-9).

In an abiding relationship, fruit grows on the vine.

Jesus Pleased the Father

I saw the Lord always in My presence; for He is at My right hand, so that I will not be shaken. Therefore my heart was glad and My tongue exulted; moreover My flesh also will live in hope; because You will not abandon My soul to Hades, nor allow Your holy one to undergo decay. You have made known to Me the ways of life; You will make Me full of gladness with Your presence (Acts 2:25-28).

I want to give you seven things from Acts 2:25-28 that Jesus used to stay in an intimate relationship with and please the Father. These also apply to our relationship with the Father and with each other. You may discover in this section the freedom and ability to walk in this sequence until you are 85 and white haired! Take a few minutes and read the entire chapter noticing the words "My" or "Me."

Vision therapy (vs. 25). "I saw the Lord always in my presence; Jesus always saw the Father in His presence, so He had some sense of vision. He conducted and behaved Himself as if He could see the Father and the Father could see Him. "Where there is no vision [no redemptive revelation of God], the people perish; but he who keeps the law [of God, which includes that of man]—blessed (happy, fortunate, and enviable) is he" (Prov. 29:18 AMP). The first step to getting in trouble is to take our eyes off Jesus. Peter was walking on the water, took his eyes off the Lord and sank. The minute we get distracted and look at the mortgage, or the sickness, or the nagging neighbor, we begin a downturn.

Spiritual strength (vs. 25). "For He is at my right hand, so that I will not be shaken." Most of us have walked with the Lord long enough to know that there are things in life that really can and do shake our bush. To name a few, betrayal, death, divorce, financial issues, and mega-failure can rock our whole foundation. David saw the Lord at his right hand and drew spiritual strength from Jesus so that he would never be shaken. When Judas betrayed Jesus, He was unshaken. When Peter betrayed Him, He was unshaken. When the whole Jewish system turned against Him, He was unshaken. The Christian life is not difficult; it is impossible. In the final analysis, Jesus puts steel up our backbone and makes us stand. It's not our will power or great prayer life. If we don't know how to draw spiritual strength, we will fall on our face, but at least we will be pointing in the right direction!

Worship (vs. 26). "Therefore my heart was glad and my tongue exulted." Worship is a vital part of being a Father-pleaser. The Lord asks for a heart of worship. 1 Corinthians 14:2 says, "For one who speaks in a tongue does not speak to men but to God; for no one understands, but in his spirit he speaks mysteries." Worshipping in other tongues is more than important; it is the source of learning to please God as a Father. Jesus was a worshiper.

Hope (vs. 26). "Moreover my flesh also will live in hope." Hope doesn't mean, "I hope it doesn't rain tomorrow;" it is something that we live for. The reason people commit suicide is because they've lost hope. Hope is a duty or a responsibility and is one of the most powerful factors in being a Father-pleaser. When we lose hope, we are in serious trouble. Like a punching bag with sand in the bottom, hope is something that keeps popping back up when you punch it. Hope is resilient. It keeps us when things get tough relationally. Obtain your hope from Jesus as Lord and then guard your hope well.

Death and resurrection (vs. 27). "Thou wilt not abandon My soul to Hades nor allow thy Holy One to undergo decay." It seems that over the past few decades increasingly fewer voices preach the Cross because we are determined to feel good. Consequently, we are experiencing cross-less Christianity. Jesus doesn't use rubber nails, but if we don't embrace death, we can never enjoy resurrection.

Because the Church has refused death, it is running out of fuel. Preaching the Cross in a legalistic manner is not what I am saying. We must learn to be careful when we hear the message of the Cross from those who only know how to speak death. There are many who are ignorant of the joy of the Cross and the end result of the release of His resurrection. Death is normal in the Christian life because it is followed by resurrection. Water baptism is a pattern of death and resurrection. Father-pleasers embrace death and resurrection as a way of life in our personal lives as well as in our relationships. When some form of death comes knocking at your door, it is the Cross. Father is asking you to embrace it in order to impart and disclose that necessary Kingdom life that comes out of death.

Leadership (vs. 26). "Thou hast made known to me, the ways of life." Leadership comes at many levels. If you're out in the bush and your eight-year-old son knows where the jeep is, he's the leader. If you know just one more thing than somebody else, you become the leader.

Leadership has both joy and responsibility. Whether you realize it or not, there are men and women in your life, perhaps at work, school, or at church who are following you. It is important to be Father-pleasers because they are watching your life and hoping that you're real. They want to believe that you know where you're going.

Satisfaction (vs. 28). "You will make me full of gladness with Your presence." Notice that in our first point we start by being in God's Presence, and we end by being in His Presence. Father-pleasers are full of joy no matter their circumstances. We live in a discontented society and the plethora of advertising makes materialism even worse. We must acquire a better model, the latest edition, the one with bells and more buttons. Rather than putting our values in spiritual matters, society pressures us to value material things. Jesus wants to satisfy something deep in us so that we will be full of gladness in His presence. Once we get our vision clear and see the Lord, we will not be shaken.

The Rewards of Waiting on God

Years ago, I went on a fast for 21 days during which I only consumed water. The purpose of the fast was to hear from God concerning His power to affect miracles in our ministry. As the end of the fast approached, however, I had not heard anything from God.

I felt as if the Bible read like a stock market report and that the Lord had moved to another state. In addition, through most of my fast I was so crabby I could have bitten the head off a nail. My wife would say from time to time, "Honey, are you sure you don't want to eat?" What she was really saying was that I was acting meaner than a junkyard dog on this fast!

I could not figure out why God was so silent. But at the very end of those 21 days, God spoke one word to me. It cost me 63 meals to get this one phrase, but it changed my life. God simply said, "Wait."

A vital aspect of our prayer life is waiting on God. Many times in the Scriptures we are told to wait. Isaiah 40:31 says, "Those who wait for the Lord will gain new strength; they will mount up with wings like eagles, they will run and not get tired, they will walk and not become weary." There are three lessons about the rewards of waiting on God here.

First, you will exchange your weakness for His strength, and that's a promise.

Second, the literal Hebrew says, "they will sprout wings." To live in the Spirit, you have to catch the currents of whatever the Holy Spirit is doing. The eagle never runs from the storm, but always flies into it.

Third, to run and not get tired has to do with living out the Christian life. Just as a race can be longer than you are conditioned for, the journey into Christian maturity can prove to be longer than you anticipated. Waiting on God will give you the strength to finish well.

Not Always Our Timetable

In Exodus 24:12 the Lord tells Moses to go up on the mountain and "remain there." So, Moses went up and waited seven days before God spoke a word to him.

An interesting aspect of the Lord's nature is that He is never late, but He rarely comes according to our timetable.

Judith and I often lived on faith for our resources. One time we had a gas bill that was thirty days late. The Lord had simply not supplied the money for that bill yet. I asked the Lord to please hurry with the money, and He replied, "The gas is not shut off yet, is it?"

That was not exactly the answer I wanted to hear. I really had no desire to wait any longer for His provision. But, if we are going to deal with God, we have to first realize that He is God. We cannot hurry Him, for that would be finding fault with Him.

Proverbs 8:34-35 says, "Blessed is the man who listens to me [wisdom], watching daily at my gates, waiting at my doorpost, for he who finds me finds life and obtains favor from the Lord." To me, this means that if I get impatient of waiting, leave, or give up prematurely, I may miss something the Lord had for me.

Another verse that has to do with waiting is Isaiah 30:18, "Therefore the Lord longs to be gracious to you, and therefore He waits on high to have compassion on you…. How blessed are all those who long [wait] for Him." The Lord longs to reveal Himself to us, but He waits for us to wait on Him. As we learn to wait on Him, He will reveal Himself to us.

Waiting intensifies our hunger for God. It's like waiting for supper. The longer I wait, the more intense the hunger becomes. As we learn to wait on God, we will find our hunger for Him increasing. Psalm 42:1 says, "As the deer pants for the water brooks, so my soul pants for Thee, O God."

He Acts as We Wait

The verse that ties together the whole topic of waiting on God and gives it new meaning is Isaiah 64:4, "From of old they have not heard nor perceived by ear, neither has the eye seen a God besides Thee, who acts in behalf of the one who waits for Him." Unfortunately, just the opposite is true for most of us. We act while the Lord waits for us.

Activity is not tantamount to spirituality. If you want God to act on your behalf, you need to learn how to wait on Him and not get involved in more and more things. There is so much activity in some churches that one would have to be in top physical condition just to be a member.

The ability to wait on God expresses our reliance upon Him. It is a form of prayer that is birthed in dependence on God and is a spiritual weapon.

Matthew 6:78 says, "And when you are praying, do not use meaningless repetition, as the Gentiles do, for they suppose that they will be heard for their many words. Therefore do not be like them; for your Father knows what you need, before you ask Him." The moment you express dependence, the Lord is able to move on your behalf. Give evidence to Him that you are waiting.

Suppose someone took me out three miles in the ocean, put me on a buoy and said, "Wait for me." I have no doubt that I would be there when he got back. But if he put me in downtown San Francisco with money in my pocket and said, "Wait for me," chances are slim that I would wait. The only reason I might wait would be if I needed him. If I am dependent, I will wait even though I have a thousand other options because I recognize God as my source. That is what God wants. But we wait on the Lord not only because we are dependent on Him but also because we love Him. Waiting on Him shows that we honestly desire to know Him and love Him in a deeper way.

Learning how to wait on God places three requirements upon us, and, if we understand them, we will be better prepared to do what pleases God.

No place to hide. The first requirement in learning to wait on God is that we must believe God is everywhere—omnipresent. Some people worry about trying to find God, but my approach is where can you go to hide from Him?

In Jeremiah 23:23-24 the Lord says, "'Am I a God who is near' declares the Lord, 'and not a God far off? Can a man hide himself in hiding places so I do not see him?' declares the Lord. 'Do I not fill the heavens and the earth?' declares the Lord?"

One of the problems you face in waiting on God is learning the difference between God being everywhere and God being here. He is omnipresent, yet at the same time, when He manifests His presence in a place, you will know it. If you have ever felt like your prayers were dripping off your chin and dropping on the floor, press through. He really is there, but He wants you to wait on Him.

One time a man called me in the middle of the night and said, "I am in desperate trouble. Will you meet me so we can talk?"

Over the phone I could hear rock music blaring in the background, and I said, "Sure, I'll come talk with you." So I got out of bed and followed his directions down to the bar where he was at the time. It was a really raunchy place. I walked in and sat down next to him.

"Aren't you afraid to be in here?" he asked.

"No, I'm not afraid to be here," I replied.

"Would the Lord come to a place like this?" he asked.

"He's here," I said. As I spoke those words, the manifest presence of the Holy Spirit was very evident.

"He is here!" the man said. He could feel the power of God in that place.

In that bar, we experienced the manifest presence of God, that sense of really knowing the Lord was right there with us. God's omnipresence is not just a fact we can know intellectually; we can also experience His presence in a tangible, undeniable way. There is no hiding from the presence of God.

Waiting expectantly. The second requirement in learning to wait on the Lord is expectancy. My friend, Ern Baxter, once told of a candy store that would sell a handful of candy for one penny. One day a little boy walked into the store and stood in front of the candy jar. After a while the candy store owner said, "Well, which one do you want?" The little boy just stood there and waited. After a few more minutes the owner said, "Well, son, make up your mind." Finally, the little boy said, "I can't make up my mind." Impatiently, the owner made the choice for him, reaching into one of the jars with his big hand grabbing the candy. The little boy had to use both hands to hold all the candy he got for his penny. He was no dummy he waited, expecting the man to act. That is the way it is with God. We wait, and He acts.

Poise your soul toward God. The third requirement in learning to wait on the Lord is that we poise our soul toward God. When we meet people, we can sometimes tell what kind of an attitude they have. Some people have their souls poised toward earthly things. Others are obviously poised toward God.

When Judith and I saw the movie "Chariots of Fire," years ago I was really moved. While we were watching it, she could tell it was affecting me, and kept saying, "Easy, Honey." She thought

I was going to prophesy right there in the movie theater. But I respond that way because when my spirit is poised towards God, inspiring scenes and events begin to move my spirit up toward Him. He is pleased when we keep ourselves poised toward Him.

Sometimes when I wake up during the night I go to my study and wait on the Lord for a while. Most of the time I do not have anything specific to pray about because I am just waiting. Usually during those times I need a Bible because my mind sometimes wanders. I'll begin thinking that I really need to have the oil changed in the car. When this happens, all I need to do is read a verse or two of Scripture, and it brings my mind back to the Lord. If the thought persists, I have a pencil and paper handy to write it down, so I can get my mind back on the Lord.

Another critical problem is dealing with distractions: telephones, kids, people, things. I walked into an office one day and construction work was going on outside with jack hammers. I said to the receptionist, "How do you put up with so much noise?"

She responded, "What noise?"

I saw immediately that when our spirit locks into God's Spirit, we are not even aware of the distractions. As I sit in the Lord's presence I say, "Lord, it's me. I know that You know I'm here." What am I doing? I am presenting myself before God, hoping He will reveal Himself to me. I am seeking the manifest presence of God.

Many times His presence just comes and draws near. I know that while I wait, God works. In fact, much of what I teach comes from the Lord during these times of waiting on Him. Judith said to me, "If people only knew how easily you come by some of the things you teach, they would be jealous." Waiting on God gives me the strength and portion I need.

Waiting Is a Skill

It is not necessary to always stop and sit down to wait on the Lord. As I walk along or drive in the car, I can be refreshed in my spirit by taking that time to wait on God. If we work at it, we come to a place where the poise of our soul is toward the Lord, and we can enjoy the Father's presence.

For years I would get up at 5:00 a.m. to wait on God. Many times as I was kneeling before the Lord, I would fall asleep and wake up at 7:00 a.m.! I would say, "Oh, Lord, I'm sorry."

The Lord said, "That's alright, I understand your desire." But, there is a big difference between desire and ability. Desire comes natural, but ability must be learned.

Jesus said to His disciples, "Pray with Me for one hour." They all fell asleep. Aren't you glad you are not the only one?

Most of us are very active. If you stopped and knelt waiting on God for very long, you know what would probably happen. If falling asleep is something you struggle with, try walking as you wait on the Lord. When I need to repent or if I am generally in a place of asking, I'll kneel. When I sit, I am in a posture of absolute dependence on God. There are many other postures for praying and waiting on Him, too.

Take time to be alone with God and learn. Poise your spirit toward Him saying, "Lord, I want to learn how to wait on You. Holy Spirit, help me experience the Father's presence." I suggest you start with five minutes then gradually move to fifteen minutes or more until you learn how to wait on God. Keep in mind that His omnipresence is there with you.

A little secret I have found useful comes out of 1 Corinthians 6:19, "Your body is the temple of the Holy Spirit." Each of us are a little church. I do not mean individualism or fragmentation, simply that no matter where you are physically, you can have your own church service in your own sanctuary. You can be waiting on God at the bus stop, in rush hour traffic, picking up the children from school, or waiting for an appointment.

Another one of my secrets that may be helpful is from 1 Corinthians 14:28, "If there is no interpreter, let him keep silent in the church; and let him speak to himself and to God." In other words, let him have his own church service. I hope I do not offend anyone, but when I go to a meeting that is a loser, I have my own little camp meeting.

Years ago, I went to a meeting and the man who was speaking said, "Hallelujah" over and over. My mind began to wander, and I started thinking about going fishing. The Lord said, "That's not a good attitude."

I said, "What am I going to do, Lord?"

He replied, "It would be better for you to pull yourself in and wait on Me." You can use the situation as an opportunity to wait on God.

I was driving down the street one day and a jogger, glistening with perspiration, was waiting for the light at the intersection to turn green. I rolled my window down and said to him, "Will you run three miles for me?" Some people think the pastor is going to do your praying and waiting for you. However, no one but you can run the three miles. You must learn for yourself how to wait on the Lord and enter His presence by faith. You must also learn to discipline your mind and deal with distractions. You can be in your own little sanctuary in one minute flat.

I would encourage you to take the time to study the many other Scriptures about waiting on God. As you find yourself waiting in His presence, your strength will be renewed, and as you wait, the Lord will act, accomplishing in you and through you all that is His purpose for you.

Summary

Within the Father, Son, and Holy Spirit there is a circle of friendship between the Trinity and we are being invited into it. When Jesus started His journey with the disciples, one of His goals was friendship—He wanted to reveal Father's secrets to them. Before He could do that, He had to work them through a few "relational" problems like calling down fire on their enemies, competing for the best positions, self-confidence, fear of man, and betrayal. When they had learned their lessons, He began to reveal His heart to them, offering them a degree of intimacy that is difficult to grasp. Real friendship involves trust and intimacy, not over-familiarity.

In this Plumbline, Bob gives us four ingredients common to friendship and to basic human need and shows us that if a relationship is always directed to you or from you, it is not reciprocal. God is calling us into a true friendship with Himself and with men and women in the body of Christ. Every one of us has developed elaborate escape mechanisms and use both self-protection and control as barriers to intimacy in our relationship with God, in our marriages, as well as in every other relationship. We know exactly what to do and say when the pressure is on. The only way we can experience intimacy is by acceptance. We must accept each other just like we are and choose to surrender self-protection and control.   When we center our whole being on pleasing the Father, it radically affects our ethical and moral behavior.

A vital aspect of our circle of friendship with God is waiting on Him. By waiting on Him we exchange our weakness for His strength. After a while, we come to a place where the poise of our soul is toward the Lord, and we can enjoy the Father's presence. Isaiah 40:31 says, "Those who wait for the Lord will gain new strength; they will mount up with wings like eagles, they will run and not get tired, they will walk and not become weary."

LIFECHANGERS ®

P.O. Box 3709 ❖   Cookeville, TN 38502
931.520.3730 ❖ lc@lifechangers.org
www.lifechangers.org

www.ingramcontent.com/pod-product-compliance
Lightning Source LLC
Chambersburg PA
CBHW071739020426
42331CB00008B/2094